# You, Me & Depression

# You, Me & Depression

## A Battle of the Heart and the Mind

ALEXANDRIA BROWN

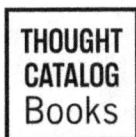

THOUGHT
CATALOG
Books

BROOKLYN, NY

THOUGHT
CATALOG
Books

Collective
World

Cover photography by © Allef Vinicius, Designed by KJ Parish.

Published by Thought Catalog Books, a publishing house owned by The Thought & Expression Co., Williamsburg, Brooklyn.

First edition, 2017

ISBN: 978-1945796739

Printed and bound in the United States.

10 9 8 7 6 5 4 3 2 1

*For you, because without you there'd be no this
and I really am glad there's this.*

*For the people in London and the people outside
who got me through this period. All my love always.*

*For Molly, for taking the time to be a part of this journey
and for always being encouraging. I owe you.*

*And for the future, God you look beautiful.*

# CONTENTS

# Foreword

**Molly Burford**

I first saw Alex's byline on Thought Catalog about a year ago and I was immediately intrigued by her writing. Her style is truly unapologetic in its vulnerability. Typically, when we think of unapologetic, we think of unabashed tones and harsh word choices, but that's not Alex. There is a stubborn sensitivity in her work that is truly impossible to forget. Her crystal clear wisdom runs around your mind long after you read her work.

What started as admiration for her craft later led to actual friendship. After sharing a few funny tweets regarding mac and cheese (obviously), Alex and I became friends. We added one another on Facebook and now talk almost daily via Messenger, as well as video chat. We talk writing, life, and everything in between. I feel truly lucky to have connected with Alex. So obviously, when Alex asked me to read through and edit her second book, as well as write the forward, I don't think I could have said "yes" any faster.

So, let's talk this second book, shall we? *You, Me, & Depression* is a story of survival, heartbreak, and resilience. It's a memoir of falling into depression and in love, at the same time. It's raw and honest. It doesn't try and cover up and glamorize depression and heartbreak. Alex shows the brutal reality that is living with depression every single day, how it follows you, no matter where you go and what point in your life you're at.

My favorite part of the book, though, is that it's a picture of depression many are afraid to paint: loving someone despite the pain in your heart and mind. Many people who suffer from depression, including myself, shy away from dating and love out of fear of being seen fully and out of fear of heartbreak. But not Alex. She fell in, head first. She loved deeply and fully despite it. And in the end, it broke her heart. But she was able to put it back together.

If you've ever been through the throes of depression or love someone who has, this book is a must read. It will help you understand the hell that is depression and the inner workings of someone's mind who fights it every single day. Alex is brave to share her story, and I know it will inspire others to share their own.

1

# the start

—

*Everything has a beginning.*

**I've started this about four different times, and each time I've hated it more.**

It's been trying, to say the least. I guess that just comes as part of the territory of being a writer. I want all my published work to be perfect and just the way I pictured it, seamlessly expressing all of my inner truths with ease and clarity. But this is hardly ever the case. Because, if I'm being honest, my truths are rarely perfect. My inner workings are a garbled mess, a mess that only I, the writer, could understand and relate to. And my depression has made this chaos even more winding and convoluted, that much more difficult to convey to you, the reader. But, since you're here with me, I'll do my best to explain.

I guess I will start with what this book is about, and why it's been so difficult to write. In short, it's about mental health; my mental health. And, what I've found is that the deeper I get into my own depression, the less I want to talk about mental health. So there's that. It's also maybe about the fact that when it got dark and really scary, I still managed to somehow also fall in love with someone else going through the exact same thing. It was weird, intense and at times completely consuming. But it didn't change the fact that while trying to take care of myself, I was also trying to take care of someone else; which is never a good idea But more on that later.

I guess what I want you to take away from my own personal bedlam is the following;

That love exists. Even in the strangest of times. It's still a very real thing that all of us have a chance to experience, at least once in our lifetimes. Can I guarantee that it's going to work out? Hell no. What I can say is that it's completely worth it.

I also want you to understand how completely crippling depression can become if you just let it march around your mind recklessly unattended. No matter how good you are at suppressing it and tucking it away, it will find a way to eat you alive, to chip away at the hope that's required to live this life. I speak from personal experience. You see, I am very good at burying things and not telling people how I'm feeling, out of fear of being labeled as weak. But that almost destroyed me. Luckily, I'm now learning that this is not something that's true. We aren't weak because of any version of mental illness. We just need a little extra help. That's all.

Finally, I want you to see yourself in these pages. Maybe you've gone through depression. Maybe you've fallen in love while depressed. Maybe you know someone who's been depressed. Or maybe you've just been in love. Either way, I want you to see yourself in my story and know that you are not alone. You are never alone no matter what you may be feeling.

I've worked hard my entire life to conceal my anxiety and depression. It almost became second nature for me to say, 'I'm fine' when I really wasn't. Do you know what's the most painful thing in the world? Starting to cry then stopping yourself. You get this giant lump in your throat as you struggle to swallow the sobs until they dissipate and your heart just hurts. It's the worst feeling but I had mastered it. I didn't want to cry and I didn't want to have a weakness.

Parts of this book isn't going to make much sense but then again sometimes mental health doesn't make sense. And love definitely doesn't make sense. These pieces are from a time in my life when everything was falling apart while I was trying so badly to hold it together. This story has a beginning, a middle and an end, like all good tales before it.

So, come along on my mental dissolution that happened while I was in some of the most beautiful places in the world. Read about how falling in love with someone managed to be the worse thing I could have ever done. See the hope that almost leaps out of the pages that someday I would be able to feel 'normal'; whatever the hell that looked like.

# 2

# you

—

*What you are and what you will forever be to me is a lesson.*
*A lesson I had to learn in order to become who I need to be.*
*So for that, I thank you.*

# Beginnings

Beginnings are weird. They just are. When you meet someone for the first time, you're instantly trying to read them. You're trying to figure out who they are and how they could potentially play a role in your life; even if you don't realize that you do it.

Our beginning wasn't special. It wasn't roses and confetti, it was natural. It was almost like when I met you I couldn't be without you after. I didn't want to be. I wanted you to be in my world because I knew you were something special. And I wasn't wrong.

It was almost like the first second I got you alone, I got to see the real you. The person brimming with the spirit that I so badly found attractive. I saw something fragile and innocent, yet strong and well versed.

Our beginning wasn't romantic. It was what it was. We met through friends. I knew if they liked you that I would too. So, our friendship was something I cherished deeply. You got me on a level that not many people did and I knew that our souls were somehow bound to each other. Maybe they weren't ever meant to intertwine but they were meant to meet.

So, I dated other people and you did too but those lunches I got to spend with you were always my favorite. They were hours I looked forward to and would smile about all day. I didn't think anything of it other than us as friends, but now looking back even then I knew. I knew that one day I was going to fall in love with you. I knew it was going to be tragic, deep and faster than I could ever imagine.

Our beginning wouldn't technically have been 'our beginning' if we were to write a love story. It would be a beginning that happened after years of knowing each other. It happened at the worst time in my life, where I debated every day as I woke up. I debated if I was going to be able to make it through the day and continue to go down the path of my life. My depression had gotten worse. And our bond? Well, it just got stronger. I never took it for granted and I never wanted it to go away.

Our beginning wasn't fireworks or hearts stopping, it was two people who really just liked each other's company. It was two people who had their hearts stomped on previously and unsure of what the future held. It was two people who felt they weren't good enough for anyone, including each other.

Can two broken people try to heal each other? Or do two broken people need to first heal then come together at a later date? At a date when they both are satisfied with their personal progress.

I had a crazy feeling at our second beginning. The one where friendship and relationship lines would be blurred. I had a feeling that maybe we needed each other to get through the fall. We needed each other to depend on because it felt like no one else got it. While I suffered through the worst part of my depression, you were there. You were there whenever I needed you to be and I could never take that away from you.

Our beginning wasn't tragic or dramatic. It was calm and calculated. It was slow and deliberate. It was everything I wanted a beginning to be. It wasn't a beginning that starts romance novels but it was ours.

Our beginning was exactly what it was meant to be.

## Prerequisites for Falling

I'm not scared to jump in and give something my all. I'm not afraid of getting hurt and I'm not afraid of telling someone how I feel.

But I am afraid to fall in love. I'm afraid to fall in love with you. I'm not afraid of a lot of things, but I am completely terrified of love with you. I'm scared that I'm going to sink into you and forget who I am. Because I've done that before and rebuilding my identity isn't something I'm willing to do again.

I could dive head first into this and tell you that I never want you to go. I could tell you all the things you need to hear to know that you are completely the one I want to be with.

**But I can't tell you I love you. I can't tell you I love you for what the weight of those words mean.**

It would mean that I am no longer one but now a part of another. While I'm already completely whole, my soul would fuse with yours and I wouldn't be able to pick up the pieces if you let go.

So, before I give in and before I fall in love with you, I need you to tell me the truth. Don't tell me you need me if you're planning on leaving. Don't tell me I'm special or different or someone you can't be without if you're waiting for the day when you can take off and not look back.

I don't believe I'd ever regret falling in love with you but before I plunge right in and put my heart on my sleeve, tell me the truth. Your truth. Tell me what you want and where you see this going because I can't take not knowing. I can't take falling only to not be caught by you when I hit the bottom.

You can't call me 'honey' or 'sweetheart' and just not mean it. You can't tell me that you see our future together when you're only planning a future on your own.

Don't lead me on. Don't tell me everything you think I need to hear to sleep with you. While sex isn't something I'm scared of giving to the wrong person, giving my love and heart is. While I can come back from a one-night stand gone wrong, I can't come back from loving someone and be unscathed for the next person.

There are seven billion people in this world and I know that I'm happier with you than anyone else. I don't need my friends to tell me that I'm already completely falling for you. I don't need them to remind me of my stance on falling in love and why I should be careful. I don't need them to remind me that my depression is so deep and finding solace in another person could potentially end disastrously.

So, just be honest. Keep me in the loop. Let me know if your heart is telling you something different. Because if you're true, then I'll be able to keep my head on straight. I'll be able to fall in love slowly until I can't imagine what not loving you is like.

So, don't tell me you need me if you don't believe that you do before I fall completely head over heels in love with everything you are.

# Edinburgh, Part I

I woke up in a cold sweat wondering what the fuck happiness was. I was in a cupboard sized room while my parents slept close by. We were in Edinburgh. I had met them for the weekend. It was two weeks since I had returned to London from Canada and I my depression had progressively gotten worse. That was two weeks since I felt the jolt of electricity that came with seeing you.

It didn't matter, though. Your constant texts could take me away from the fact that I was falling deeper into a depressive state I wasn't sure I'd ever get back from. It was painful. It was like someone pricking my skin over and over again while telling me how I wasn't worth it.

I was in a cold sweat at 3 AM. I wanted to stop listening to the demons that were telling me I was worthless but I couldn't. I managed to fake it for another few hours until my parents woke up. I managed to keep the words at bay and haul my ass out of bed in order to pretend to be normal. The truth was the week before I had seen my parents, I hadn't been showering as often as it was socially acceptable or eating much of anything really. I had managed to somehow pretend that I was doing OK even though they knew I wasn't.

An hour later, in the streets of Edinburgh with my two favorite people ahead of me, I asked myself again if this is what happiness felt like. I started to cry uncontrollably. My knees started to buckle and I tried to conceal the fact that I was having a total breakdown behind my parents. When my dad turned around and saw me crying, I could see the confusion on his face. It didn't make sense why my life that seemed so perfect was so quickly crumbling in my hands.

It's because depression doesn't make sense. If there's one thing I know it's that. I don't know the reasons why sometimes everything's OK and the next I'm profusely crying on a sidewalk. I don't understand why I was in one of the most beautiful places in the world and I couldn't figure out how to get my breathing under control. I couldn't begin to talk about what was wrong because I had zero ideas how to make my brain comprehend that this should be happiness.

Except I wasn't. I wasn't happy. I hadn't been happy in a while.

But then, there was you. The only thing that had made me feel anything other than sad. It was never a good idea to fully invest in someone without any guarantees. But I did anyway.

I don't really understand how it happened, but there you were. You made getting up in the morning a little easier. You made it so I didn't feel absolutely crazy. You made me start to feel a bit closer to me again. While I bawled to my parents about how my depression had completely overtaken me, you were still in the back of my mind as my cheerleader.

So, thank you. Thank you for seeing the real me in times I couldn't find myself. I needed you to be something and you were. You were exactly what I needed.

## Who are you?

So, let's talk about you.

Who are 'you,' exactly? I could describe you in so many ways, both positive and negative, and I'm still not sure I'd ever get it all completely right. You are an enigma wrapped in a mystery that made me want to peel away your layers to reveal the only thing I was one hundred percent sure of; your raw and beautiful heart.

You were every single thing I wanted in someone and simultaneously everything I didn't want. You're smart. You're funny. You're handsome. You're kind. You're sensitive. You're forgiving. You're selfish. You're narcissistic. You're a little broken.

You are a lot of words that contradict each other. And maybe that's the best way to describe you; a complete contradiction. I don't think you've ever lied but you weren't good at telling the truth. You were always there but at the same time completely aloof. You are so incredibly smart but also so incredibly dumb it drove me insane.

But I loved you.

I loved you because you are who you are. To me, that was enough. You exactly the way you are is the exact way that I want to love you. I don't need perfect because I am so unbelievably flawed myself.

I saw your demons. God do they haunt you. They tell you you're not good enough. Those same demons haunt me. The thing is that you're always striving for perfection. Your idea of perfection is having the perfect car, girlfriend, house, job and life purpose. But perfect doesn't exist. Still, it didn't stop me from trying to be perfect for you.

Because I loved you.

That's what it comes back to every time. Love. Being in love with you. Being in love with you instead of trying to fall in love myself.

But this isn't about me. It's about you.

Who are you really? I want to dive into you and be able to give a description that's completely fitting but I can't. I can give an overview but when it comes right down to who you are, I can't because I don't even think you know who you are.

I could use metaphors to describe you, but all I really need to say is this: you were there for me. It's odd when someone becomes the reason for you to get out of bed, but you were that.

So how did I fall in love with you? That's something I'm still trying to figure out. I'm still trying to sort through how one minute you were just someone in my life to someone I couldn't see not in my life. It's upside down and backward in my brain. I've tried to make sense of it but now I've stopped.

I've stopped because what I do know is this; I loved you.

And maybe that's enough. Maybe that's all I need to know about you. Maybe that's all I need to say to explain who you are and what you did for me.

## The Cure

Want to hear something embarrassing? I want to be your cure.

I want to be the one who makes it so whatever is plaguing you just goes away. I wanted to be the person you could turn to in those hard moments and cling too in order to know that you're OK. That you're going to be OK.

But it doesn't work that way. You can't fix another person, especially when you're struggling yourself. You can't love someone into being whole.

You can love them all you want, but ultimately it comes down to them. You're fighting an uphill battle trying to get someone else to see their value that is so blinding to you. This is what you taught me anyway. I could write word after word describing how crazy in love with you I was but it won't do anything because you don't love you.

Which fucking flabbergasts me. It does. It makes me so confused how someone like you can't see how much you have to offer the world. These expectations you put on yourself aren't goals to live up to, they're hindrances that are making it hard for you to even live.

I hated when you would say you don't deserve me as if I'm something that is better than anyone else. When it comes down to it, we're all just people trying to figure our shit out. It doesn't matter if you're rich or gorgeous, you will struggle. Everyone struggles. It's just the way life works.

So, I listen to you compare yourself to others. I listen to you fully believe you're not good enough. I listen to you talk about everyone else like they're so much better than you. And I feel the pain that you must feel in order to convince yourself that it's true.

I have nothing to really offer you other than momentarily brilliant bits of wisdom, complete love and trust. I can't really give you the finer things in life but I can be there for you in those moments when you can't love yourself. I wanted to fix you with my love. But you can't fix another person with love.

But I have nothing to offer you except love.

I promise I'll always be there. I will be the person that gets you through anything and always be the person you can rely on. It doesn't matter what happens with this or us, I'm not going anywhere.

No matter what, I'll be your cure.

## How You Got Me Through My Worst

People told me that as my depression got worse, I needed to focus on myself. I needed to figure my shit out before possibly being able to meet someone who would be able to understand but I didn't do that. I fell hard and fast when I was in the darkest times of my depression.

While I do agree that we need to be in a good place with ourselves to find a love that's going to last, without you in my life I don't know if I would have gotten through those dark days. I don't know if I would have been able to understand that the things I found completely unlovable about myself were things that you didn't find weaknesses.

I've battled on my own but it was almost like a strong hand to hold when you showed up. Even still, I had bad days after we connected because overall my depression is just that, my depression. I wish I could pass the burden along and make it so that this heavy load sometimes isn't so heavy. Maybe that's why falling in love with you at that time was so easy. You made it so I didn't have to worry. I didn't have to hide things from you because you just got it.

Those are moments I could have never gotten if I had chosen to be cautious and stay away. If I had chosen to focus on myself and not let you into the deepest parts of my soul, then I would have had to do this all on my own. While I'm great with handling things on my own, you are that support to just lift me through those battles I can't fight by myself.

I sit in bed wondering about why I was cursed with this illness. Why do I have to suffer through each day trying to convince myself that life is worth living and that I'm worth loving? That's the thing about finding someone to love when you don't love yourself: you can't believe that they would ever love you back.

So, I struggle daily with not telling you that this thing we have going on is over. I struggle with missing you and completely hating you for making me face my demons daily. I know that in order to make this work, I have to be willing to see my depression and anxiety as something that I can control and not let myself feel like a victim.

What does this mean for me? It means that I must remember to take my antidepressants so there the bad days are fewer than the good. I need to go to counseling to talk about those painful memories in order for me to make new ones with you. I have to tell my story to people so that it becomes less and less a stigma in my mind.

Because in doing all of this and admitting my shortcomings, it allowed me to love you more. It allowed me to accept my faults and to see that you are only human. I can put you on a pedestal and tell you that you're better than me but that would only allow you to fall because no one is perfect. We all have our struggles. You've just chosen to help me with mine and I've chosen to help you with yours.

So maybe you've come at a time where I should be focusing on myself. Maybe you showed up at a time when my heart is completely cracked and in need of major repair.

But thank you for sticking this out with me. Thank you for trying to navigate my moods and listen to me when I panic. Hell, just thank you for everything.

## Unraveling

It happened so quickly I couldn't catch the end of the rope before it fell through my hands.

Whatever it was we had was quickly starting to fall to pieces, and I wanted so badly to stop it. But I couldn't. I didn't want to seem weak so I hid my true feelings. I pretended to be a rock even though my depression was slowly causing me to feel the worthlessness I had been pushing aside. I was the calm in your storm but the hurricane in my own.

I never felt good enough for you. I could say that over and over again and it probably won't make sense to many people. What was it about you that made me feel like I wasn't adding up? Honestly, nothing. You didn't make me feel this way. You didn't give me depression or tell me I was the worst. You did nothing other than exist in my realm as a source of happiness.

But I saw this starting to unravel and the cracks that I was pretending weren't there started to get bigger. Cracks in the foundation are the main way that a house falls apart. And, shit, was this falling apart. I loved you so much that instead of dealing with anything logical, I just wanted to do whatever I could to hold on to you.

I was desperate. No one ever wants to admit that they were acting in desperation but I sure was. I wasn't ready to lose my source of good in a time when everything was dark. But you were running as fast as you could and telling yourself the reasons why you wouldn't be happy with me.

I think we always see when a relationship is starting to breakdown. I think we ignore the major red flags that tell us to get out as quickly as possible. We ignore them because loneli-ness is a killer. I didn't want to be so lonely again. I didn't want to remember how bad it felt to be completely on my own.

I was strong and independent. I built a life for myself and worked hard to make all of the things I wanted come to fruition. But that was lonely. And I was starting to get scared that if I didn't let someone in and let someone see the real me, that love was going to pass me by. Not only that, that I was going to wake up one day and realize that everything I had built for myself wasn't enough to replace the love from another person.

So, I was desperate but just because I was, doesn't belittle who you are. When you showed up again in my life, you weren't just someone to fill the hole. You were the best thing I could have ever imagined. You got my jokes. You loved talking about books, music and cute animals. You were different in the best kind of way.

Still, it wasn't enough to keep pushing through to make this work. While I battled with my depression daily, you also had your own things you needed to work out. If we had gotten our shit together and worked on ourselves separately, this wouldn't have started to fall apart so quickly.

So, all of the expectations and love I once had for you started to unravel and with it, so did the small hope that love was ever going to be a possibility for me.

# That Night

I don't need to remind you of the night that is permanently seared into our brains. I don't need to tell you the trauma it caused me. I don't need to tell you that since that moment, I have stopped believing in love. Because you know all of that. You know the collateral damage you caused because of your own selfishness.

I don't need to tell you how I waited for you. I watched how each hour ticked on and looked at the unanswered texts I had sent you. I started to panic. Even though I knew you were just blowing me off, I thought maybe you were actually in trouble. I texted my friends. I texted our mutual friends. I asked them what to think of it all because this wasn't you. It was out of character.

But then again, it was completely in character. You never wanted to deal with situations that were difficult. You wanted to block out any sort of emotions that could potentially cause other people pain because you are a coward. It's gutless to not just be honest with someone.

So, while I worried about you, where were you?

The fuck if I know. I still don't know to this day what you were doing instead of just telling me the truth. I could probably guess though. It probably involved guilt and worthlessness and reminding yourself how terrible of a person you are.

While ultimately, this was the 'easy route' it clearly wasn't. We both have to now pick up the pieces of shattered hearts and rebuild them on their own. I have to deal with pieces of dishonesty, confusion and not being good enough. You have to deal with being a liar, a coward and feeling completely worthless.

Either way, when you made the decision to walk away and not even acknowledge the wounds that you would be causing, was when you made the biggest mistake. Because you didn't just have to deal with what you had done, you forced me to also have to deal with it.

It was the biggest betrayal of my life. Someone I had told my deepest and darkest secrets too had vanished. Like I wasn't worth a shitty excuse. I was someone who didn't deserve to be acknowledged at all.

And am I supposed to just get on with my life after that? Am I supposed to smooth over this bump in the road and act like it wasn't completely devastating? Am I supposed to go on have normal relationships with people who allegedly deserve me even though you didn't respect me enough to tell me the truth?

Go fuck yourself. Don't tell me you did this to protect me when you did it to protect you. Don't fucking tell me that I will be OK in the long run with someone else because right now I never want to let another person even that close to my heart again. I don't want someone else to take advantage of my feelings and use them to make themselves feel better.

What you did was inexcusable. What you did was completely fucked up. What you did made it so I will never be able to fully believe in love anymore.

But I forgive you. I forgive you for that night. I forgive you for the feelings since. I forgive you because ultimately at the end of the day, forgiving you is less about you and more about me.

That night changed my life in many ways and has forever

altered the way I do things. But it happened the way it was supposed too even if it did hurt.

# Record Stores

I can't go into record stores anymore.

It sounds stupid that I can't do it but it's almost like a physical recoil when I try to push up a door I've opened so many times before. I think it's because in Munich, I found that record that reminded me of you. I found that record that made my heart beat really fast and excitement explode from my chest.

It's odd how an object can cause such ecstasy but when I saw it, I saw you. And the thought of you always made me smile. I knew it was the right record because the picture etched into the front cover was exactly the ones that were permanently marked on your arm. Those pictures that I've imagined my fingers running over in exploration.

I bought it because I knew what it would mean to you and in turn that meant a lot to me. All I ever wanted was for you to be happy.

But unfortunately, I can't say that you wanted me to be happy. Because if you did, if you really truly fucking cared about me, you would have told me the truth long ago. You would have told me that the feelings I had for you weren't even close to being returned.

You wouldn't say that you were too worried to tell me the truth because of the state of depression that I was in. You would have known that honesty was always going to be the right way to handle this and I would have gotten over you much faster if you had been.

I don't trust anyone anymore. I trust the people in my inner circle and my amazing friends but I don't know if I'll ever be able to trust someone else again with my feelings. And to be honest, that frightens me.

No, that down right scares the hell out of me.

I'm not cynical. I'm not angry. I'm just defeated. You defeated me. You managed to do something that I never thought could ever happen and crush the only hope of love left in me. I know that this might be hard for you to know but at the same time I don't fucking care anymore. I don't care how you feel because you didn't care how I felt.

I could list all the ways you let me down but that wouldn't be fair. I also let myself down when I fell for you at a time I shouldn't have.

Yes, my depression was bad. Yes, my life was not going to plan. But you were the one thing that felt right.

So, we can sit here and pretend we don't know why we're not together but I do know. I know that I wasn't enough for you. I wasn't enough because I wasn't perfect. I wasn't perfect mentally, emotionally and definitely not physically.

I'm not angry that you felt I wasn't enough, I'm sad. I'm sad that I lost you. I'm sad I lost me. I'm sad that I can't go back to the beginning and choose to not ever do this with you.

Because if there's one thing in this world I regret, it's telling you the truth about my feelings. Maybe it's selfish to say, or maybe I should have protected myself better. Either way, in loving you, I set myself back when it comes to my self-worth and progress in finding happiness with myself.

While I know this is mostly your issue, it doesn't change that all the words you didn't say were written all over your face.

I can't go into record stores anymore for a fear that I could see you in another record. I can't see you and feel like all the progress I thought I made was actually all in my head.

I can't go into a record store and remember that even though I've buried it beneath a lot of alcohol and work, that maybe I still love you. Even though we will never be. We will never be what I had hoped so I avoid record stores and records altogether.

## Our End

It's odd having to write an ending when the beginning was so hopeful. After all, that's what beginnings are; full of hope. They're filled with moments of passion and feelings of butterflies and fireworks. Beginnings are not being able to live without someone, and losing yourself fully to the possibility that this time, it's finally going to work out.

But then, it doesn't. Doors slam shut. Futures are no longer visible on the horizon. Feelings are tossed aside, as though they weigh nothing. And as for the one person you thought could never break your heart? They do anyway.

It was abrupt. It wasn't an ending I saw coming. I tried to forgive you after everything but I just couldn't. I wasn't ready. I wasn't ready to let you back in after you so quickly cut me off and left. So I didn't want anything more from you because I couldn't let you hurt me anymore.

Our ending left me feeling vacant and alone. It left me confused and in pain. Our fall has been the hardest one of my life. But the worst part of it all is that you're not gone, not really. There was no clean break. There is no easy way to just not want you around. There is no easy way to erase you from my heart.

And after our end, it was two months of silence. It was two months of hot baths where I'd let my face sink beneath the water to cry. It was a January of cynicism and a February of negativity while pretending to be happy for my friends and their loves. It wasn't that I wasn't happy for them, it was just that I couldn't get over my own pain in order to fully celebrate with them.

And after those two months of deafening quiet, there was a night of screaming solitude, where all I could think about was you. You're something I just can't leave alone, like a scab I shouldn't pick at, but I do. Every single time. So, I reached out. Because I was lonely at 3 AM and not strong enough to keep myself from typing out those words. The ones that made me feel completely weak and incredibly pathetic.

Then I saw you again. Two months later, after all of the disaster, you were sitting across from me at one of my favorite places. You were sitting across from me because I couldn't just leave it where it fell. I needed something more. I needed to know what happened. I needed to know what your excuses were. I needed you pretty white lies so that I could move on from what had happened.

I listened while you told me your version of the truth. The one that made it sound like you were trying to protect me. The one where you told me you missed me and I told you I missed you too. The one that asked me, selfishly, if we could go back to our friendship, the one before all of the messiness.

That's when it hit me.

You never cared about me at all. Not in the same way that I cared about you. You led me down a path that I should have never gone down. I thought you were standing beside me but really you were always three steps ahead of me.

I tried to secure your mask before my own and that's why I'm the one who's struggling to breathe.

In counseling, my counselor warned me what would happen if instead of dealing with my issues, I took yours on. My back isn't strong enough to hold both of our problems but I still tried. I broke my back for you while you never even lifted a finger. Because if you did, you would know how heavy this all has been.

I know you want me in your life. I know I'm not someone you're going to easily replace. But what does that mean for me? You keep me around temporarily until you meet someone else? Am I supposed to be the filler partner until you meet the one you're supposed to be with?

I keep holding on. Not because I hope you'll end up realizing you love me but because I can't let go. Every night before I go to sleep, I pray for my soul to come back to me because it's still wrapped around your fingers.

Those two months without you felt like something was missing. I woke up, I had a routine and then I went to bed. I got a dog because I thought it would take away the missing you. And while he's the best thing that's ever happened to me, he doesn't replace you.

But this is the end. The end of ever believing you would be who I wanted you to be. This is me giving up the expectations that I once had. This is me saying goodbye to the person I loved so fully and intensely that it scared me.

Every ending is a beginning for something new. And am I ever ready for something new.

3

# depression

—

*Hello, darkness, my old friend.*

## Welcome, Depression

One pill, two pill, three pill, STOP. Doctors always tell you what the repercussions are of taking more than the recommended daily dose of medication. But what they're not aware of is that I'm actually not afraid of dying. No, I'm more of afraid of continuing to live. I'm afraid where this path will go if I continue to breathe and feel. That's a scary reality to live in.

I'm more scared of being alive than being dead.

It's not something I want to admit or something I talk about but it's true. It's true that sometimes when I wake up, I'm disappointed. I'm disappointed I have to live another day feeling like there is something inherently wrong with me. I'm tired of feeling like there's nothing that can change this cycle of feeling completely lost.

I thought falling in love with someone else would rescue me. It's stupid to say and even stupider to believe. Because love doesn't save you unless it's love for yourself.

And I can tell you now that loving myself is a battle I go through daily. It's because I don't value myself. I don't value my place on this Earth. I doubt where I belong and who I am. I don't know anymore.

My brain tells me just to end it. My brain then tells me to take my medication and go to counseling. It's a back and forth that I can't seem to keep up with.

My day starts out with a pep talk trying to get myself out to bed. If out of some miracle I manage to get up, I then make my way to the bathroom. I stare at myself in the mirror where I tell myself all of those mean things that you would never want to say to you. Then I cry. It's a silent cry that causes every muscle in my entire body to seize up. It's the cry that makes you feel weak and makes you wonder if you can handle this.

Then I go to work. I go to work and put a smile on my face. It sounds like it's so easy to do but I know I make it look easy. Because in my mind, I'm playing a part. A part that hides people from experiencing the scary side of my depression. I act happy and natural when really my soul is screaming 'you're so fake.'

In case you were wondering, faking it is draining. Faking it takes every ounce of energy that I have and it makes it hard to do anything else.

When I get home, I lay fetal on the couch. I collapse in exhaustion. I don't want to talk to anyone. I don't want to eat.

But the weird thing is that I don't sleep. I don't sleep because I'm up all night worrying about what I had done the day before. I worry that maybe someone had seen beneath my mask and saw that maybe, just maybe, everything isn't actually perfect for me.

If I pretend everything is perfect, then maybe it actually will be. Instead of dealing with things, all I want to do is just not. I want to be able to get through the day without having to convince myself that this life is worth living.

So I take my medication. The recommended dose. I talk to my counselor about the things that are plaguing me. In hopes that one day, this feeling of pain will just go away.

But until relief is a reality, I keep battling through each and every day.

## Dear Depression

Can I just start by saying fuck you? Really. Just fuck you. If you could just not be a thing in my life I would love that so much. But here you are and here's me. We're intertwined in each other and it's starting to make me realize that maybe there really is no escaping you. Maybe you're meant to be a part of me no matter what.

Remember that day we spent in Paris? The one where I cowered under my sheets. I didn't want to see anything. I didn't want to be around crowds. I just kept listening to your whispers that made me remember how worthless I am. I listened to you talk me into crying all day and worrying if I had made the wrong decision to leave home.

You make me feel ashamed of myself. Is that the wrong thing to say? That you're the reason why I'm so ashamed of my past and the things I've done in my life to get away from you? Those nights I woke up with someone new because I couldn't be alone with my thoughts were completely soul crushing. The nights I'd drink too much to drown out your taunting and callous words were some of my worst. I just needed to get a temporary high in order to shake you.

You've taken everything that was once beautiful in my life and made it dark and gritty. All of the things in my life that were once so beautiful are now things I question. I question when someone likes me. I question when I fall in love with someone. I question if I'm good at my job. I question if I'm a good enough friend or family member. Everything in my life is now one big question instead of just believing in myself and who I am.

Let's not forget your best friend anxiety. Fuck. Both of you together are a toxic mix. On one hand, there are days where I don't care enough about myself or anything else. But those other days when your friend anxiety visits, those days I'm hyper sensitive and care way too much about all of the outside factors in my life.

You make me feel like vulnerability is a weakness.

You make me scared to fall in love. You make me frightened that I am not going to be able to have someone love me in those dark moments. I want to be able to express my emotions without thinking that they're not valid. I want to be able to stand in front of someone and say this is a part of me but it's not all of me.

I don't want you to exist anymore. I don't want to have bad days when I can't get out of bed and instead of owning up to you, I pretend I had the stomach flu. It's embarrassing because everyone knows I'm lying but they think I'm just trying to skip out on work. They don't know that the silent demons I fight every day are worse than any stomach flu could be.

Because really, when it comes to you, you make me wonder if living each and every day is worth it. And that's scary. You make me question whether or not my life is worth it. You make me wonder if I can do this. You make me have to convince myself that I can make it through another day.

You make me take a lot of things good I have in my life for granted.

And I really fucking hate you for that. I truly do.

# Edinburgh – Part II

Edinburgh was the place where my world started to shift really fast. I figured out that happiness was something that was starting to become more fleeting than real. I saw my dad's heart on his sleeve and I knew the pain that I was causing both my parents was becoming unbearable. My pain wasn't just my pain anymore.

I had finally let it out. I had finally let my feelings of worthlessness, depression, anxiety and just mind numbing pain fall out of my mouth. I finally decided that I couldn't carry this on my back anymore without letting someone else see it. I needed them. I needed them to be there for me because I couldn't do it anymore. I couldn't see a reason to exist. While I was falling in love with someone who gave me a spark of hope, it wasn't always enough.

My heart had become dark and twisted. It was filled with an aching I couldn't really describe and one that managed to cripple my entire being. I was becoming withdrawn. I was becoming angry. I was becoming self-loathing. I was becoming my own enemy. It was scary.

Hating yourself is one of the hardest things anyone can go through. You're struggling to see a purpose to your life and everything is disgustingly dim. Why would anyone else in this world care about who you are or who you'll become if you don't even give a shit anymore?

Depression is a nasty passenger to have riding shotgun with you on this ride. While we all have many times where we feel imperfect, depression is whispering in your ears scenarios as to why you're the worst.

But you aren't the worst. I wasn't the worst.

So I stood in Edinburgh, weak from trying to fight my depression, reaching out for help because there was really no other option. I was tired of wondering what would happen if I stepped off the platform and get hit by the tube. I was ashamed of feeling fake and faking my happiness all over my social media pages instead of being real. I was no longer able to smile at everything that happened in my life, no matter how awful it was.

My life was no longer the picture perfect photograph I had masterfully photoshopped together. It was a disastrous puzzle that was in 1000 pieces all around me. Instead of letting them sit there, I had two choices; fight or give in.

But I couldn't fight it on my own. So in a tiny apartment in Edinburgh, Scotland, I let my parents in. I let them see the tortured parts of my soul I had been hiding from everyone. I let them know that even though there were huge amounts of people who loved me, I couldn't understand why. I couldn't understand when people would tell me how great I was because when I looked in the mirror, I saw someone who was 25 and a complete and utter screw-up.

My self-loathing became something I was so used to that instead of pretending it wasn't there, I started letting it talk for me. Statements that fell from my mouth filled with pessimism and pain were a more frequent occurrence. I stopped feeling embarrassed about being an asshole and just embraced the fact that I hated everything. I hated everything because I hated me.

When I let that pain talk to me, I started to see what I needed to do. I started to see how I was going to heal. I started to see the real me again. The one that doesn't give up on herself even though her world is crashing down.

In Edinburgh, with my parents, I started the battle to get back to me.

# How to Love Me Through my Depression

I'm scared my mental illness makes me unlovable. It's a statement I hate writing and a sentence I hate thinking about. But it's how I feel. And as my depression and anxiety become more chronic, my thoughts about falling in love become more negative and my belief of the chances of it happening for me start to grow slim. While I know this is a small part of me, I can't help but feel as though there is a giant neon sign following me, warning people away.

The truth is when I tell the people I'm dating it usually starts out OK. They seem to understand and accept this is a part of me, but it isn't all me. But the further we get down the path of being together and the more they realize how much it actually affects my everyday life, that is when I see them start to look for the exit.

I've had exes tell me they can't make me feel better because I'm letting these 'issues' consume me. I've had exes tell me they don't feel as though they can tell me the truth about things because they're worried it'll send me into a tailspin. I've had exes try to tell me how to manage my illnesses even though they've never experienced it themselves.

I don't need someone to tell me what to do or how to do it when it comes to depression or anxiety. All I want, all I truly want, is someone just to love me through it. That's the part that is sometimes lost on potential partners. I don't need someone to fix me. I go to therapy. I take my medication. I work hard each and every day to ensure I am doing all I can to prevent the bad days from occurring more often than not.

What I do need is for someone to just be there when things get hard. When those bad days come on and I can't think of a reason why I should get out of bed, I want someone to be there to just tell me I can do it. I want someone to hold me when, in the middle of the night, I can't breathe because my anxiety is out of control. I want to be able to tell someone my deepest darkest secrets when it comes to my illness and not have them look at me like I have three heads.

I know it's not easy to ask someone to be a part of my life when most of the time my moods are a little unpredictable. I know it's not fair that I'm going to let someone down because I just can't help myself from wanting to hide from the world on really bad days. I feel it's not reasonable that sometimes my problems become their problems because I just need someone to shoulder a bit of the weight that comes with depression and anxiety.

I know all of these things but it doesn't mean I'm unlovable or incapable of giving love. Because I so am. I know I am.

I will love the shit out of people despite the fact it's sometimes hard to love myself. I am able to listen and accept criticism when things just aren't working for my partner. I am able to just be there for someone when they're having a really, really bad day. And I'm able to empathize, not sympathize or compare when talking to someone about their problems.

So, I've been with people who don't get me or my mental health. I've been with people who have told me that my mental illness makes it so it's difficult to love me. I've also been the person pushing people away in order to protect myself from them potentially leaving me when it gets a little too hard to deal with.

But no one is perfect, and I am no exception.

# What I Learned When My Depression Followed Me Around The World

Depression follows you everywhere you go. I've been trying to outrun mine for as long as I can remember. So when it hit me in some of the most beautiful places in the world, I was left wondering if this was what happiness felt like.

**Maybe life was just a constant gray instead of living in full color.**

I spent a full day in bed in Paris, France. Instead of seeing the beautiful sites, I opted to cower under the sheets in my rental, wondering how the hell I had gotten here. I was wondering what happened in my life that made me feel like I wasn't worth love.

I hiked up a mountain in Granada, Spain. Instead of looking out at the most amazing view I've ever seen with two people I love dearly, I was wondering how quickly I could get down. I was wondering how quickly I could hide away from the world again. I wanted to sleep. I was just too tired of being in my own head.

I couldn't leave my apartment in Vienna, Austria. I wanted to see the sites. I wanted to see everything that Vienna had to offer but instead, I stayed in the apartment I rented and thought about how unappreciative I was. I was the worst person for having all of these opportunities and completely wasting them.

I got lost in my own head in Popoyo, Nicaragua. I had to sit with myself in extreme silence and pay attention to all of those disgusting thoughts I had managed to push away for so long. I heard the deep insecurities that were plaguing me and I realized there that I was broken. I was broken and I wasn't going to be able to fix it. I wasn't going to fix it because I really just didn't care about myself anymore.

I thought about how my family and friends would be better off without me in London, England. I just wanted to not be around anymore. I didn't want people to rely on me. I didn't want to care about anyone else's feelings. I wanted to be completely alone and I didn't want anyone to know what I was doing. I was retreating inside myself and even though I could see it, I couldn't stop it.

I made major mistakes in Calgary, Canada. It was home but when I took a quick escape from Europe to see my people, I made old mistakes. The old mistakes led me to remember that I am not a good person. I'm impulsive and I'm all for instant gratification without thinking my actions through. It's because I didn't care. I just wanted to stop feeling like something was missing.

I tried to heal in Geneva, Switzerland. I tried to let myself think that things were starting to get better. I had friends. I was starting over. I was getting to a place where I could be myself again. I felt like maybe, just maybe, my hopelessness was gone and I didn't have to worry anymore. I didn't have to worry about being sad because this temporary relief felt great.

I had a breakdown in Edinburgh, Scotland. After thinking that maybe things were starting to get better, I was walking through the streets of one of the most beautiful places in the world with two people I love more than anything and all I could think was, "Is this it?" I didn't feel anything inside. I didn't feel happy. I felt like for the rest of my life I was going to live half alive. I was going to just have to deal with that fact that happiness isn't for everyone. So I cried. And I couldn't stop crying for multiple hours.

I had a major anxiety attack in Bordeaux, France. I felt it build in my chest. I had been on antidepressants for one week. So when the anxiety hit, I was woken from my sleep in a panic. I started to move around the hotel room with an energy I wasn't even sure where it came from. My brain was bouncing back from telling me to calm down to telling me to freak out. I felt like I couldn't breathe. I just needed to get out of that room.

And I healed (really healed) in Brighton, United Kingdom. After weeks of therapy, weeks of antidepressants, weeks of not knowing if I was going to overcome my mental illness, I started to feel better. I saw the fog start to lift. I felt the pain of constantly hating yourself start to dissipate. I felt that getting out of bed wasn't such a brutal chore anymore. I finally started finding myself again, with a lot of help from other people.

I've taken my depression to some of the most beautiful places in the world. I've let it rule my decisions for the last while. Depression and anxiety aren't a joke. They're not something someone pretends to have to be on trend. Depression and anxiety are real and they hurt.

They take the most amazing things and turn them into something you fear or hate.

I didn't deal with my mental health soon enough. I should have done it earlier but I also learned a lot about it over those months and destinations. I know who I am now. I know that depression isn't going to rule my life anymore. I just hope that if you are where I was, that you know that you're going to be OK. That you should reach out to someone and let them know where you're at.

You are loved. You will get through this.

# Truth Be Told, My Depression Does Define Me

My depression tells me that I am broken.

It's a sentence that's been repeating through my head for the past few days. I'm broken. My heart is broken. My soul is broken. My spirit feels like it is irrevocably broken as well. I feel as though this upward climb that I've been fighting through has just gotten steeper and I, myself, have gotten weaker. I battle through each day with a smile on my face for fear that if someone sees the pain underneath, they'd see the real me.

I talk to my depression like it's another person. It visits me from time to time and I never know how long it's going to stay. We get into arguments and we battle constantly over who is going to prevail. I keep saying it's me but right now I'm not sure if it is.

I break so easily on things that I never thought would hurt me. I miss a time when I used to get through the day without an Ativan. I miss not having to remember to take my antidepressants every day. I miss not feeling like getting out of bed was a war and that my feelings weren't a burden.

**Because right now, my feelings *do* feel like a burden.** I feel like I can't be honest with people without them worrying that I'm going to do something rash. I'm tired of depression being this big piece of me that I have to constantly admit to. It's something that I just want to keep hidden away and not let define me.

But the truth is that my depression does define me. It's a part of me, a huge part. It contributes to all of my decisions and my strong paranoia of not being good enough.

When I start dating people, I have to tell them the reason I don't have more than one glass of wine is because it screws up my antidepressants. I can't just say that one sentence without the follow-up explanation as to why I'm on antidepressants.

I hate feeling fragile. I hate the way someone looks at me after I tell them about my depression. I hate feeling as though something is inherently wrong with me even though deep down inside I feel like something's wrong.

My mom once asked would it be the worst thing to be on antidepressants for the rest of my life? It wouldn't be the worst thing but then it's admitting that this is a chronic mental illness I will battle with for the rest of my life. I don't want to think of it as something that I can't cure because I don't want to believe in its longevity.

But there's a really weird thing that happens every once in awhile when I share my story. I meet other people feeling the exact same way. I meet people who feel guilty that the depression makes things feel 100 times worse than they actually are. I meet people who feel as though while there really isn't anything wrong in their life, they just can't seem to be happy.

**That's the thing about depression, there's no real reason to have it, you just do. It's a part of your brain. It is something that is for some reason your reality. It's mine, too.**

So I get through the bad days trying to remember that even though my brain is telling me I'm broken or that there's something wrong with me, there really isn't. I have a little bit of a harder battle than some but a little easier of a battle than others.

You can't compare your struggles to anyone. You can't let your mental illness tell you you're worthless. You need to find the inner strength you've found this far and pull from it when the days get tough.

Depression is a part of me but it doesn't own me. It doesn't own you either.

**Not now. Not ever.**

# Healing

I know how weird this is going to be to say, but there has been so much healing out of the pain my depression has caused. My depression has seen me do some pretty crazy things in order to heal but nothing really worked. Nothing worked until I let myself be.

What do I mean by let myself be?

I started to admit that I had a problem. Not just to myself, but out loud. I stopped pretending the random outburst of anger or tears were just out of frustration. I started to realize that these were signals that something was going wrong within, rather than situational

And so, I stopped blaming others for my issues. I used to point fingers to my first love for causing me the pain in my heart that made it hard for me to move on. I attributed feelings of inadequacy at my job to my old bosses. I said it was my parents' fault for not giving me the tools to really grow up. I blamed everyone and everything I could in order to not have to look inwards.

Because what's going on inwards is so fucking dark.

It just is. It feels awful. You actually have to sit and listen to yourself and your pain. And then, you have to figure out the tools that will help you get through this, through this paralyzing, all-encompassing madness.

For a while, I used love as a tool. I fell in deep, real love despite my depression. And while he helped me see a lot of things in me I needed to fix within myself, he didn't know what to do when I was on the brink. He didn't know how to tell me he wasn't ready. He just didn't know how to love me through my depression.

And honestly, that set me back. The " healing" I thought I was seeing came to a screeching halt the very second he walked away. The depression came back in full force. in all its ugly, deafening quiet. But, let's be real; it never really left. I was only fooling myself. Instead of listening to all of the fibers of my being screaming out to just focus on me, I decided to focus on him. But all I was doing was distracting myself from the real issues.

It was no one else's issue. No matter how badly I wanted to blame everyone else.

Depression doesn't make you a bad person. It doesn't make you a weak person either. It's a mental illness that manages to take everything great in your world and crush it. Depression is doubt, pain and worthlessness all wrapped together in one punch.

I can't tell you I'm better, not really. It's been months since I started this journey and there are still days I wonder what the fuck I'm doing. I still have days where getting out of bed is the biggest chore I have of the day. I still feel like a breakdown is coming even though it seems as though things are starting to finally feel a bit better.

All I know is that healing is a path that you travel down and not necessarily has an end destination. It's a constant battle and a twisty road that will keep you guessing. But that doesn't mean you don't keep going.

And in all honestly, you do heal on this confusing path. You do heal when you find yourself looking in the mirror and seeing in your face that you're ready to beat this, that you're ready to tell depression to pack its bags and never come back. And this won't be easy, and it will sometimes feel awkward and all that. And other times, it will be downright fucking scary. But I know if I'm able to embark on this messy thing called healing, so can you. After all, we've waded and battled through depression. We've survived so far.

Who's to say we can't heal, too?

## Bye, Depression

Saying goodbye to my depression is more of a dream than a reality. There hasn't been a quick fix for me and I'm not sure I believe a quick fix exists.

Depression most of the time feels like an uphill battle. A battle that is literally live or die. Because if you lose, well, there's no coming back from that. Depression is the hardest opponent you will ever face because it just doesn't give up. Ever.

You could be fine one day and then the next, *boom!* you're on your back on your floor crying profusely, wondering if this life is worth living. There's no way to predict these moments and it's not something easily explained to the outside world.

Because you're not sick in a way people can see. No. You're sick in a way that makes it easy to judge. You're sick in a way that makes you look lazy and unmotivated. You're sick in a way that makes people think asking, "But why can't you just be happy?" is a reasonable question. Like this is all some choice.

And it sucks. It sucks to have defend that fact that you feel a constant pain in your heart, day in and day out. It sucks that you feel like you need to tell people that you have the stomach flu instead of the actual truth that you really just can't leave your apartment today. You can't tell people that everything just feels grey in a world of color without you getting looked at like you're insane.

But know what? You're not insane.

Just because life is tougher for you than someone who doesn't struggle with depression, doesn't mean you're insane. It doesn't mean you're crazy. It doesn't mean you're less than anyone else. It just means that you have something different about you, a different kind of battle.

I used to hate when my mother used to tell me I was different. I didn't want to be different. I wanted to be the same as everyone else, but my depression and anxiety always made me feel like a bit of an outsider. So I tried harder. I tried as hard as I fucking could to fit in and I succeeded. I succeeded with pretending that everything was so great.

I succeeded until I wasn't strong enough to pretend anymore.

And then it was time to deal with it. It was time to have a breakdown and go on stress leave. It was time to admit to the world that I am not OK and I wasn't going to hide it anymore. I wasn't going to post on Facebook that my life was going amazingly when it really wasn't.

I wasn't going to feed into my own false reality anymore.

Maybe I can't say goodbye to depression, but I am saying goodbye to the person who used to hide it. The person I am now can tell you that the best decision I've made is admitting that I wasn't OK.

So I'm saying goodbye to the person I was before and embrace the new one I am now. The girl who has depression but is fully accepting this piece of her. It's a piece of her she is determined to not let win.

And *damn* does that feel good.

# 4

# me

—

*Because you should always be*
*the main character in your story, right?*

## To the People I Owe Everything To

How can you talk about yourself without mentioning the people who made you who you are? I was lucky enough to be born into a family that supports each other, loves each other and does anything for each other.

But I felt like I was a burden on them for the longest time. I was always the black sheep. They're all smart in sciences and math, while I always wanted to be a writer. They're all successful and I always feel like I'm still trying to find myself. They're good at being in control of their feelings, whereas I'm a tsunami just waiting to explode on people.

They are the best part of me for many different reasons.

Without them, I wouldn't have survived the fall. When my knees buckled in the middle of Brighton station after the worst panic attack of my life, my mom was the one on the other line trying to get me to a place where I could breathe again. She has been my rock time and time again.

When I suffered one of the worst hurts to date, my brother and sister in law were the two people who messaged me to make sure I was OK. My brother spent nights talking to me to make reassure me that just because I had quit my job, that I wasn't a loser. He made me promise I wouldn't get back into another situation that wasn't good for me until I got better. All he wanted was to see me OK again.

My dad started to call me every day to check in on me. Every day. Every single day. If you knew my dad, you'd know that he is not a phone person. But he made sure to call me so I knew that I wasn't alone, no matter how it felt right now.

How do you talk about yourself without mentioning the people who made you who you are? You don't. You remind them how much they mean to you, not only when you're going through the tough shit, but also when you're doing OK. You tell them you love them and if it wasn't for them you don't know where you'd be.

I can't write about myself without mentioning the people who raised me. While my parents and brother did most of the work, my friends who've been there through everything and still manage to try to hold me together when I'm falling apart deserve a shout out too.

In those dark moments, when I'm not sure who I am anymore or what my place is, those people are the ones who are there building me up when nothing feels right.

So this is a love letter to those people I need the most in the times when I can't see my own worth. I love you.

# London

When I decided to leave London, it was one of those decisions that felt like something I would regret. I was living a life that I had dreamed of. I had great friends. I was doing everything a 25-year-old could ever want or desire. I was seeing different places and learning about different cultures.

But I wasn't happy. I wasn't happy because there were so many things under the surface that were plaguing me. And I thought I could push through. I had always been good at pushing through, after all. I had always been good at burying things that felt painful. I had just been so good at pretending for a long time.

But then I couldn't pretend anymore. I couldn't walk through the day pretending that I wasn't thinking about what would happen if I died. It was a scary thought that all I wanted to do was not exist anymore. I just couldn't do it. I didn't want to do it.

This was before I owned up to my depression and anxiety as more than just the blues and nerves. I realized that maybe I needed help.

There were a lot of things that led me to this place. Bad breakups, bad jobs and all around bad situations where I felt like I wasn't in control of anything. I had always lived my life as if things happened to me and I had zero control over the situation.

I have always been the person who cares way too much about everything. I'm always the person who's 100 percent in when it comes to dating. I'm always the person who wants to hear everyone's opinion on a situation before I make a decision. I'm the person who will work as hard as possible at my job, even if I hate it.

So, I was scared when London started to feel more and more like the wrong place for me. I was scared when my job started draining me to the point that I just laid on my couch after and cried. I was scared when the person in London that used to give me relief from the everyday stress, my roommate, was asked to move out of our flat. It was feeling like my friends felt like I was a burden even though I know they didn't feel that way.

London was everything I thought it was going to be and more. But it also taught me that I needed to make decisions based on what was going on with *me.*

My depression had gotten to a point that was too much for me to handle without the comforts of my home. Home isn't necessarily a place, but you get that warm feeling in your stomach. And, shit, was that feeling missing for me.

But instead of moving home, I moved to Brighton, a town on the English Channel. I tried to forge through and be happy. The sea did a great job of making me feel a little closer to home. But then again, it still wasn't home.

And then I had a breakdown at work and in front of people. It was the most vulnerable moment in my life. I just couldn't do it anymore. I needed to find out who I was and needed to get back to me.

So, I took six weeks off for stress leave to begin healing. Those six weeks consisted of me changing medications, weekly counseling and spending time with just myself. My doctor and therapist gave me one rule: I had to leave the house every day.

For people with depression and anxiety, you will understand how incredibly hard that is. It's one of the most monumental tasks when it shouldn't be that big of a deal. The first five days,

I didn't leave my house once. Not one time did I feel the need or desire to leave my house. I had the worst anxiety of my life and I hadn't been eating much.

However, slowly but surely, I got more and more perspective on my situation. The medications started to work. The therapy started to help. I started to leave the house just so I could do things that I wanted to do. For once, I didn't feel like I owed anything to anyone except myself.

Then I decided it was time to go back to Canada. That decision remains the hardest and most complicated decision I had ever made. There are days I wonder what life would have been like if I had stayed. But somewhere in my heart of hearts, I knew I needed to go.

And that is the one thing I'm still sure of till this day.

## Restart

My life changed the second I got off the plane back in Canada. Everything I thought I would have when I got back was magically gone in a week. I was lucky to have one of my best friends welcomed me into her home while I waited for my apartment to be finished. When I landed, I thought I would feel instant relief from everything that had been tormenting me.

But it didn't happen that way.

I had no job. I lived alone on an air mattress. I had nothing to look forward to. What's worse is I lost the person I thought I was going to be able to start fresh with. Even though I was in the place I wanted to be in the whole world, I wasn't happy still.

That's because running doesn't make you happy. Leaving a place in order to escape yourself just isn't a realistic expectation. You take you everywhere you go.

So, I sat in my bathtub. I cried. I applied for jobs. I took the comments from people who said, "Well *you* weren't gone very long." Those same people were the ones I told I was never coming back to. The ones I had hugged goodbye for so long because I wasn't sure I was going to see them again anytime soon. Who knew that in nine months I'd be sitting across from them in the same old places we used to frequent before.

Slowly but surely, instead of my depression getting better, it got worse. It got so fucking bad I thought about what this world would be like without me.

Then things started to move fast. I found a job. My parents bought me a bed. And then I got myself a dog. Roscoe.

In a moment of pure loneliness, I decided it was time to stop waiting for someone to rescue me and start to rescue myself. Which meant doing the things that I had always wanted to do without worrying what the fuck other people thought. I had lived my entire life trying to do the right thing or the cool thing and I was done trying to be whatever the hell the invisible audience in my head thought I should be.

Then something magical happened. I started to attract people into my life that gave me things that I would never have learned otherwise. My friendships with the people I had known for a long time got deeper because I let them see darker parts of me.

I thought I was never going to fall for someone again. Then I did. Not only did I fall for someone, he gives me the best gift anyone could give another person. He lets me be me. In every single form. While nothing is perfect, I know that he has been one of the greatest people to come into my world.

When I decided I needed to find a therapist, I stopped looking for one in the traditional sense. I looked for one that I knew would be right for me. And I found one. One that's incredibly smart and funny. One that makes it easy for me to open up to. One that is my very own cheerleader and I feel like is completely on my side.

All of these wonderful things started to happen even as the bad continued. Those good moments are enough for me to continue to feel like I'm starting to become me again.

# Never Settle for 'Unsure' Love

I believe in love. I always have and I'm pretty sure I always will. Even though there have been times in my life I have claimed I was done with the idea of it. The truth was, I was just done trying with people and I was done pretending that maybe love was going to be a thing for me.

My mom has said that I have always been a hopeless romantic. Ever since I was a child, all I ever wanted to do was be married. I wanted to meet someone and just know instantly that they were the one for me. I wanted them to feel the same way.

I thought this was reality and when I met my first love at 18, I was so sure I had found it. I believed I was one of those lucky people who magically found love early. I loved him deeply and intensely. It was the kind of love I always thought it was going to be. Except it actually wasn't. While I loved him, he wasn't ready.

That could be the title of my autobiography: 'I Fell In Love With Someone Who Wasn't Ready.' Because that would be the definition of my entire love life until this point. I keep falling for people who aren't ready. And it doesn't make them bad people. It doesn't make them assholes. It simply makes them human.

Love is scary. If there's anything I've learned in 26 years, it's that love is completely and utterly terrifying. You have to trust someone with your most precious gifts: your heart, soul and body. You have to trust they're going to take them and nurture them. You have to trust they're not going to crush the things that make you, well, you. You have to believe them when they say they're going to be there for you. You have to be vulnerable and open up about things that still pain you.

I don't think I hold anger towards any of the men in my past. I know they all have caused pieces of my self-doubt and insecurity, but I also know it's something that I need to work on for me. Not for anyone else.

I love fully and deeply. The kind of love that people sometimes believe is fake. But it's not. I'm a witness to it. My love is acceptance of people for who they are. It's being someone's refuge. This world is so full of hate and pain that if I can be someone's solace then I'm going to be. I lose myself to others. I lose myself in love.

And my friends don't understand. They worry about me. They see what happens when a relationship ends after I've done everything I could to save it. I know they listen to me cry and wonder what the fuck I had done to cause another person to leave. They hurt for me and with me. I know these things. I know I could probably take a different approach.

But that's just not me. That's not how I love. And, I could never stop loving people.

I love all people, in many different ways. I've fallen in love two times in my life. Both of them ended disastrously and had caused me to wonder what I wasn't good enough to find my other half. And that's when I realized my problem.

I didn't need someone to complete me. I'm already whole; cracked and broken, but whole. I don't need another half, I need someone to be my partner, my best friend and my confidante. I need someone who complements me. I don't need someone to show up, save me and make all of my issues OK. That's not what happens in real life. **And that's not what love is, at least the kind of love I want.**

The truth about life is that we're all a bunch of broken people trying to find ourselves and people to love all of our brokenness. We are people who look at every flaw we have, every crack and use them as excuses as to why we're unlovable.

I'm a hopeless romantic, but I'm waiting for someone who will be 100 percent sure that they want to be with me. I'm done chasing. I'm done playing with timing. Instead, I am going to wait for the person who one day is ready to not only listen to me when I'm at my worst points of my depression but is there to love me no matter what.

Promise me you won't settle for half love. And love yourself fully for everything you have to offer. Then, there's no way you can lose.

## To the Person Who Loves Me Next

There are so many different ways to start this. I could tell you that everything is magically fixed and I am going to be OK with going with the flow, but that's a lie. While I've been working on taking care of myself and managing my depression better, I know that there will be times where I spiral back down. I know there are times my anxiety is going to make me sick to my stomach and you're not going to understand how to fix it.

I promise you that you don't have to. I know it will be difficult to watch me go through the pain and struggle that comes along with these mental health issues but I promise you that all you have to do is listen to me. I don't need you to take care of me and put your life on pause. I just need you to hold me a little tighter and tell me how much you love me.

I can't promise you that my love isn't going to be intense. I can't promise that I won't do everything in my power to make you happy. I will support every single one of your dreams. I will love you in those moments you feel completely unlovable. I will believe in you no matter what because of that love.

I am going to be so proud of you. Every moment and every step of the way. I am going to be your biggest cheerleader and push you when you need to be pushed. Just like I know that when I need the same thing, you're going to be in my corner.

I don't want you to change anything about yourself. While you're not perfect, I know that neither am I, so don't change for me. Change for you. If you want to. Any sort of up and down you go through, I am going to be there to hold your hand.

I've done a lot of things in my life that I am not proud of. I've done things that have made my friends question my sanity and my parents question their parenting choices. But none of that was anyone's fault. It was me learning to be me. It was me letting go of what I thought I should be and realize what I could be.

I don't want you to ever question how much I feel for you. It's going to take me a bit to trust you but that doesn't mean it's never going to happen. I've trusted a lot of people and not all of them have been worthy of it. I know you are.

I'm still a work in progress and I probably will be for my entire life. So I'm so glad you've chosen to make me a part of your life as not only your love but also as your best friend.

Whatever this will be and whoever we will be together and apart, I want you to know that I'm not going anywhere. Not today. Not tomorrow. Not ever.

So thank you for letting me love you and thank you for loving me in return.

5

# what's next

—

*Where do we go from here?*

This past week I suffered a major anxiety attack, one that has to be my worst to date. I cried in my boss's office, I tried to push away someone super important to me in an attempt to look strong and I had made some pretty overall bad life choices just to feel better.

I know things are getting bad when I stop eating and sleep seems to be as likely as unicorns. And shit were things getting bad. But I did the exact same thing I did before. I pretended that everything was OK. I didn't want to burden the people around me with what was going on. Even though I learned that opening up and being vulnerable was a good thing, it still wasn't something that felt natural.

So, I didn't. Not for a bit, anyway.

I was so scared that if I let someone see my demons again that they were going to leave. Then I decided I needed to. I needed to tell someone, or else I wasn't going to be able to deal with it.

What I've learned over the past few months is that it's easier to carry the weight of these illnesses if I have people beside me, encouraging me the way. But I realized people can't be there for me unless I let them.

My advice is and has always been, open up to someone. Anyone you trust enough to help you. If you don't feel as though you have that in your life, there are so many professionals willing to assist you through this dark time.

Just know that I believe in you. I know that you can do this. I know that you need to understand what your purpose is and I wish could give you a concrete answer. What I do know is that you have a purpose on this Earth. So hang on to that in your darkest moments when you feel like you are and have nothing.

I don't think I can predict what's next. I know I can't. No one can. All I can do is hope that I continue to work on myself and win my battle with depression. I'll have setbacks and I'll have times where I don't know if I believe in myself anymore. I also know that I can get through this. I can battle every day in order to try to get my mental health under control. I have to remember my worth in those dark times.

Whoever and wherever you are, just know that you are so loved and you will get through this.

# About the Author

Alex spent the last year being depressed in some of the most beautiful places in the world. Through this journey, she fell in love not only with someone else but with herself. Being diagnosed with depression and anxiety, Alex has been through the highs and lows that come with each disease. Even though she doesn't have it all figured out, she's still trying to make it through each and every day stronger than the last.